DAYS OF
HEAVEN ON EARTH
PRAYER AND CONFESSION GUIDE

A Prayer Guide to the Days Ahead

BY KEVIN L. ZADAI

TABLE OF CONTENTS

Author's Note and Special Thanks

---◦◊◦---

In addition to sharing my story with everyone through the book, Days of Heaven on Earth: A Guide to the Days Ahead, the Lord gave me a commission to produce this book, Prayers and Confessions for Days of Heaven on Earth: A Prayer Guide to the Days Ahead. It is a prayer and confession book concerning the areas that Jesus reviewed and revealed to me during several visitations. I want to thank everyone who has encouraged me, assisted me, and prayed for me during the writing of this work including Dr. Jesse and Cathy Duplantis. Special thanks to my wife Kathi, for her love and dedication to the Lord and me. Special thanks as well to all my friends who know how to pray and receive Heavenly Visitation.

1

THE PROMISE OF HEAVEN ON EARTH PRAYERS AND CONFESSIONS

LORD,

I trust in You and do what is right in Your eyes. I fix my heart on Your promises. My God, I will be secure, feasting on Your faithfulness. I make You the utmost delight and pleasure of my life, and You will provide for me what I desire the most. I give You the right to direct My life. As I trust You along the way I will see You "pull it off" perfectly for me!

HOLY SPIRIT,

I thank You that you reveal the future and make it my present remedy, to get me prepared so that my enemy is disarmed before the situation even develops.

FATHER,

I need to abandon my own understanding about my life and its difficulties and run to You. I pursue You and attach myself to You. You will take me where I need to go! I refuse to let go of You until I get to my *"Days of Heaven on Earth"*!

HOLY SPIRIT,

I allow the love of the Father and the Son to permeate me as I receive my healing now. Revelation from You, the Holy Spirit, confirms Your truth to me in the name of Jesus! The Father and the Son will come and make Their home with me. I open my heart's door
and watch the Trinity move in to stay!

LORD,

it is supernatural that I can pull down demonic strongholds, using spiritual weapons of truth (sword of the Spirit which is the Word of God), and bring down anything a demon says, or inspires man to say, that exalts itself above the knowledge that You gave me! My weapons are not carnal. I will use the example of You Jesus, Who used the Word of God against the devil in the desert during His temptation. You responded every time with, "It is written!"

LORD JESUS,

You are my Victorious Warrior Who went before me to conquer Satan.
I must remember to do what You did. You were the Son of God and
the Son of man. In temptation You said, "It is written," to the enemy,
and I will do the same!

FATHER,

therefore shall I lay up these, Your words, in my heart and in my soul, and bind them for a sign upon my hand, that they may be as frontlets between my eyes. And I shall teach them my children, speaking of them when I sit in my house, and when I walk by the way, when I lie down, and when I rise up. And I shall write them upon the door posts of my house, and upon my gates: That my days may be multiplied, and the days of my children, in the land which the You LORD swore unto my fathers to give them, as the days of Heaven upon the earth. For if I shall diligently keep all these command-ments which You command me, to do them, to love You LORD my God, to

walk in all Your ways, and to cleave unto You; Then will You, the LORD, drive out all these nations from before me, and I shall possess greater nations and mightier than myself. Every place whereon the soles of my feet shall tread shall be mine: from the wilderness and Lebanon, from the river, the river Euphrates, even unto the uttermost sea shall your coast be. There shall no man be able to stand before me: for the LORD my God shall lay the fear of me and the dread of me upon all the land that ye shall tread upon, as You hath said unto me. Behold, You set before me this day a blessing and a curse; A blessing, if I obey the commandments of
the LORD my God, which You command me this day.
(see Deuteronomy 11:18-27 KJV)

HOLY SPIRIT,
I know the Word that God speaks is alive and full of power [making it active, operative, energizing, and effective]; it is sharper than any two-edged sword, penetrating to the dividing line of the breath of life (soul) and [the immortal] spirit, and of joints and marrow [of the deepest parts of my nature], exposing and sifting and analyzing and judging
the very thoughts and purposes of my heart.
(see Hebrews 4:12 AMP)

FATHER,
I know that if anyone is in Christ, he is a new creation; old things have passed away; behold, all things have become new.
(see 2 Corinthians 5:16-17 NKJV)

JESUS,
by the mercies of God, I present my body a living sacrifice, holy, acceptable to You, which is my reasonable service. And I am not conformed to this world, but am transformed by the renewing of my mind, that I may prove what is that good and acceptable and perfect will of God.
(see Romans 12:1-2 NKJV)

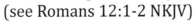

HOLY SPIRIT,

for though I walk in the flesh, I do not war according to the flesh. For the weapons of my warfare are not carnal but mighty in God for pulling down strongholds, casting down arguments and every high thing that exalts itself against the knowledge of God, bringing every thought into captivity to the obedience of Christ, and being ready to punish all disobedience when my obedience is fulfilled.
(see 2 Corinthians 10:3-6 NKJV)

JESUS,

You asked the religious leaders, "why do you not understand My speech?" Because they are not able to listen to Your word. They are of their father the devil, and the desires of their father they want to do. He (the devil) was a murderer from the beginning, and does not stand in the truth, because there is no truth in him. When he speaks a lie, he speaks from his own resources, for he is a liar and the father of it. But because You tell the truth, they (the religious leaders) do not believe You.
(see John 8:43-45 NKJV)

FATHER,

Jesus was led up of the Spirit into the wilderness to be tempted of the devil. And when he had fasted forty days and forty nights, he was afterward an hungred. And when the tempter came to him, he said, If thou be the Son of God, command that these stones be made bread. But he answered and said, It is written, Man shall not live by bread alone, but by every word that proceedeth out of the mouth of God. Then the devil taketh him up into the holy city, and setteth him on a pinnacle of the temple, And saith unto him, If thou be the Son of God, cast thyself down: for it is written, He shall give his angels charge concerning thee: and in their hands they shall bear thee up, lest at any time thou dash thy foot against a stone. Jesus said unto him, It is written again, Thou shalt not tempt the Lord thy God. Again, the devil taketh him up into an exceeding high mountain, and sheweth him all the

Kingdoms of the world, and the glory of them; And saith unto him, All these things will I give thee, if thou wilt fall down and worship me. Then saith Jesus unto him, Get thee hence, Satan: for it is written, Thou shalt worship the Lord thy God, and him only shalt thou serve. Then the devil leaveth him, and, behold, angels came and ministered unto him. Father, when I am tempted, I do what Jesus did, using the word of God against the Devil. Afterward, angels come and minister to me as well.
(see Matthew 4:1-11 KJV)

FATHER,

Jesus said to them, "All of you will be made to stumble because of Me this night, for it is written: 'I will strike the Shepherd, and the sheep of the flock will be scattered.' But after I have been raised, I will go before you to Galilee." Peter answered and said to Him, "Even if all are made to stumble because of You, I will never be made to stumble." Jesus said to him, "Assuredly, I say to you that this night, before the rooster crows, you will deny Me three times." Peter said to Him, "Even if I have to die with You, I will not deny You." And so said all the disciples.
Father, by your Holy Spirit, give me a heartfelt reality of who You are. Then, I will be faithful to You until the very end of my life.
(see Matthew 26:31-35 NKJV)

JESUS,

when You had eaten breakfast, You said to Simon Peter, "Simon, son of Jonah, do you love Me more than these?" Peter said to You, "Yes, Lord; You know that I love You." You said to him, "Feed My lambs." You said to him again a second time, "Simon, son of Jonah, do you love Me?" He said to You, "Yes, Lord; You know that I love You." You said to him, "Tend My sheep." You said to him the third time, "Simon, son of Jonah, do you love Me?" Peter was grieved because You said to him the third time, "Do you love Me? "And he said to You, "Lord, You know all things; You know that I love You." You said to him, "Feed My sheep." *Jesus I will feed your sheep faithfully!*
(see John 21:15-17 NKJV)

JESUS,

You told me, "If you love Me, keep My commandments. And I will pray the Father, and He will give you another Helper, that He may abide with you forever—the Spirit of truth, whom the world cannot receive, because it neither sees Him nor knows Him; but you know Him, for He dwells with you and will be in you. I will not leave you orphans; I will come to you."
"A little while longer and the world will see Me no more, but you will see Me. Because I live, you will live also. At that day you will know that I am in My Father, and you in Me, and I in you. He who has My commandments and keeps them, it is he who loves Me. And he who loves Me will be loved by My Father, and I will love him and manifest Myself to him."
Judas (not Iscariot) said to You, "Lord, how is it that You will manifest Yourself to us, and not to the world?" Jesus, You answered and said to him, "If anyone loves Me, he will keep My word; and My Father will love him, and We will come to him and make Our home with him. He who does not love Me does not keep My words; and the word which you hear is not Mine but the Fathers who sent Me." (see John 14:15-24 NKJV)

FATHER,

I keep trusting in You, the Lord, and do what is right in Your eyes. I fix my heart on Your promises, God and I will be secure, feasting on Your faithfulness. I make You the utmost delight and pleasure of My life, and You will provide for me what I desire the most. I give You the right to direct my life, and as I trust You along the way I'll find You pulled it off perfectly!
(see Psalms 37:4-5 (TPT)The Passion Translation)

FATHER,

I trust in You, LORD with all my heart, and lean not on my own understanding; In all my ways acknowledge You, and You shall direct my paths
(see Proverbs 3:5-6 NKJV)

2

THE PERSONALITY OF JESUS PRAYERS AND CONFESSIONS

I ENDURE LONG

JESUS,

You are committed to me. You have the ability to stay in the situation with me for a long time. You suffered greatly for me, and during that suffering, You maintained Your position to ensure the punishment for my sins was complete. I know of the suffering that You endured for me and I am amazed at Your Love that allowed and strengthened You to *ENDURE SUCH PAIN AND HARDSHIP* for me. It is beyond my ability to comprehend. **Therefore, I ENDURE LONG!**

I AM PATIENT

JESUS,

I must accept that I am not perfect like You, Who are without sin. I will never be good enough on my own. I am enthralled with Your patience for me during my journey with You. You understand my inability to comprehend certain truths. That is why You spend so much time teaching me through the Holy Spirit. You want me to live in the truth (reality). When I fail, You are patient with me and understand my weaknesses because You lived in a body as well. **Therefore, I AM PATIENT!**

I AM KIND

JESUS,

what can I say? You are the kindest person I have ever met. This is one of the main reasons why I want to come and be with You in Heaven. Why would I want to be away from the kindest person in the universe? You are very direct, but kind at the same time. **Therefore, I AM KIND!**

I AM SELFLESS

JESUS,

every time I encounter You, You are thinking about me! When You ask me to do something for You, it is ultimately for someone else that You are considering. You take care of Your people. You do not need anything. You want to give me what You have. **Therefore, I AM SELFLESS!**

I LOVE JUSTICE

JESUS,

I know You will address situations concerning me that need justice. You WILL MAKE IT RIGHT ON MY BEHALF. I will stay out of the way by walking in forgiveness with everyone and justice will come swiftly. You have a very large Law enforcement department comprised of angels at Your disposal and they are armed. Also, You know the Judge. Jesus, our Father is the Head Judge of the Universe! **Therefore, I LOVE JUSTICE!**

I LOVE TRUTH

JESUS,

the Word says that the truth will set me free. Lord Jesus, when You speak, it is always the truth. You love to see people get free and worship. You smile when You see truth reigning because that was Your Mission on the earth. You were sent to tell the truth about the Father and His Kingdom and set people free! You SAW SATAN FALL LIKE LIGHTNING! **Therefore, I LOVE TRUTH!**

I AM COMPASSIONATE

JESUS,

many times You had compassion on the people and healed them. You always want to help. I recognize that I do not know what to do in some situations so I cry out to You and You hear me. Other times I am silent, and You still hear and answer me. I am dear to You. **Therefore, I AM COMPASSIONATE!**

I LOVE RIGHTEOUSNESS

JESUS,

You love the righteous ways of the Father. Everything in the universe was set in righteousness. Now, through the mighty work of salvation, I am waiting for the kingdoms of this world to become the Kingdoms of my God. You will reign as King over all the earth. **Therefore, I LOVE RIGHTEOUSNESS!**

I BEAR UP UNDER ANYTHING

JESUS,

You have proven that You can bear the sins of the world. I know that You can bear my burden also! I cast all my cares upon You, for You care for me (1 Peter 5:7)! I take Your yoke upon me and learn from You, for You are gentle and lowly in heart, and I will find rest for my soul. For Your yoke is easy and Your burden is light (Matthew 11:29–30). **Therefore, I BEAR UP UNDER ANYTHING!**

I BELIEVE THE BEST FOR MYSELF

JESUS,

the time I spend with You makes me know that not only do You want the best for me, but You also believe the best of me. Lord, very few people understand this, thank You for revelation of this truth: You are for me and You do not doubt me. I'm telling you, Lord, I get this: I am set free! **Therefore, I BELIEVE THE BEST FOR MYSELF AND OF MYSELF!**

I BELIEVE THE BEST FOR EVERYONE

JESUS,

You are looking for faith. As soon as You find faith, You answer it. When I discern who You are and what You have done for me, I begin to speak and act out Your intentions. At this point, all of Heaven jumps in, and I will begin to have *Days of Heaven on Earth*. I will allow you to use me to build up my fellow believers and see them have *Days of Heaven on Earth* as well. **Therefore, I BELIEVE THE BEST FOR EVERYONE!**

I AM HUMBLE

JESUS,

being humble does not mean I am weak. I have never once thought that You were weak. You are very strong but very wise. You will let me do what I want if I choose to find out the hard way, or I can ask for Your help and it will come quickly. I always ask now, and my life is getting easier. Being humble is being wise. **Therefore, I AM HUMBLE!**

I AM CONFIDENT

JESUS,

being confident in You is not being prideful; it is called submission. Also, being confident in You is humility! Humility is wisdom. Jesus, You always do the will of the Father and that brings confidence! I am humbly wise in You. **Therefore, I AM CONFIDENT!**

I PAY NO ATTENTION TO A SUFFERED WRONG

JESUS,

You have seen it all, and yet You still ask, "What can I do for you? My plans for you are awesome!" You asked the Father to forgive those who crucified You (see Luke 23:34)! I repent and let offences go! My miracle is coming. **Therefore, I PAY NO ATTENTION TO A SUFFERED WRONG!**

I AM YIELDING TO HIS GOODNESS

JESUS,

I do not despise the riches of Your goodness, forbearance, and longsuffering, and know that the goodness of God leads me to repentance (Romans 2:3–4). Every time I have a visit with You, I end up repenting. You are that good! **Therefore, I AM YIELDING TO YOUR GOODNESS.**

I AM FAITHFULL

JESUS,

You truly are a friend that sticks closer than a brother. Even when I am faithless, You are still faithful because that is who You are as a person all the time. You are always there for Your own. **Therefore, I AM FAITHFULL!**

I AM GENTLE

JESUS,

gentleness is not weakness. You bring peace and trust because You are so gentle. When the Spirit is moving, I sense Your gentleness leading me. **Therefore, I AM GENTLE!**

I AM SELF-CONTROLLED

JESUS,

You teach about self-control. One of us has to have it all together at all times, and You have this one mastered. I do not to let myself be distracted by the flesh or evil spirits. **Therefore, I AM SELF-CONTROLLED.**

I AM HOLY

JESUS,

You are HOLY. There is no one like You! There are no words for You are the HOLY ONE. Better to encounter Your Holiness with Your blood applied. You are Holy! Period! Your blood has made me HOLY. **Therefore, I AM HOLY!**

I AM BOLD

JESUS,

You can suddenly become as bold as a lion after being as gentle as a dove! When I spend time around You in the Days of Heaven on the Earth, I realize that I need massive amounts of healing and deliverance. When I acknowledge this, I will receive. Jesus, You will work me over good and send me out whole and ready to minister to others. I am ready! Your ministry, Lord, is coming forth! **Therefore, I AM BOLD!**

I AM A MIGHTY WARRIOR

JESUS,

You will go forth like a mighty man, You will rouse up Your zealous indignation and vengeance like a warrior; You will cry, yes, You will shout aloud, You will do mightily against Your enemies (Isaiah 42:13 AMP). Therefore, Jesus, I will go forth like a mighty man, I will rouse up Your zealous indignation and vengeance like a warrior; I will cry, yes, I will shout aloud, I will do mightily against my enemies. **Therefore, I AM A MIGHTY WARRIOR.**

HOLY SPIRIT,

God is a Spirit (a spiritual Being) and those who worship Him must worship Him in spirit and in truth (reality). (see John 4:24 AMP)

JESUS,

"For where two or three are gathered together in Your name, You are there in the midst of them." (see Matthew 18:20 NKJV)

FATHER,

love endures long and is patient and kind; love never is envious nor boils over with jealousy, is not boastful or vainglorious, does not display itself haughtily. It is not conceited (arrogant and inflated with pride); it is not rude (unmannerly) and does not act unbecomingly. Love (God's love in us) does not insist on its own rights or its own way, for it is not self-seeking; it is not touchy or fretful or resentful; it takes no account of the evil done to it [it pays no attention to a suffered wrong]. It does not rejoice at injustice and unrighteousness, but rejoices when right and truth prevail. Love bears up under anything and everything that comes, is ever ready to believe the best of every person, its hopes are fadeless under all circumstances, and it endures everything [without weakening]. Love never fails [never fades out or becomes obsolete or comes to an end]. (see 1 Corinthians 13:4-8 AMP)

HOLY SPIRIT,

Your fruit (of the Spirit) is love, joy, peace, longsuffering, kindness, goodness, faithfulness, gentleness, self-control. (see Galatians 5:22-23 NKJV)

HOLY SPIRIT,

Your fruit (of the Spirit) is in all goodness, righteousness, and truth. (see Ephesians 5:9 NKJV)

JESUS,

You said that when the Spirit of Truth (the Truth-giving Spirit) comes, He will guide me into all the Truth (the whole, full Truth). For He will not speak His own message [on His own authority]; but He will tell whatever He hears [from the Father; He will give the message that has been given to Him], and He will announce and declare to me the things that are to come [that will happen in the future]. (see John 16:13 AMP)

JESUS,

You said to the people who believed in You, "You are truly my disciples if you keep obeying my teachings. And you will know the truth, and the truth will set you free." (see John 8:31-32 NLT)

JESUS,

You told me, "I saw Satan falling from Heaven as a flash of lightning! And I have given you authority over all the power of the enemy and you can walk among snakes and scorpions and crush them. Nothing will injure you. But do not rejoice just because evil spirits obey you; rejoice because your name is registered as a citizen of Heaven." (see Luke 10:18-20 NLT)

FATHER,

I am waiting for the seventh angel to sound: "And there were loud voices in Heaven, saying, "The kingdoms of this world have become the kingdoms of our Lord and of His Christ, and He shall reign forever and ever!" And the twenty-four elders who sat before God on their thrones fell on their faces and worshiped God." (see Revelation 11:15-16 NKJV)

HOLY SPIRIT,

Therefore I humble myself under the mighty hand of God, that He may exalt me in due time, casting all my care upon Him, for He cares for me.
(see 1 Peter 5:6-7 NKJV)

JESUS,

You tell me to take Your yoke upon me and learn of You, for You are gentle (meek) and humble (lowly) in heart, and I will find rest (relief and ease and refreshment and recreation and blessed quiet) for my soul. [Jeremiah 6:16.] For Your yoke is wholesome (useful, good—not harsh, hard, sharp, or pressing, but comfortable, gracious, and pleasant), and Your burden is light and easy to be borne. (see Matthew 11:29-30 AMP)

FATHER,

Jesus prayed, Father, forgive them, for they know not what they do. And they divided His garments and distributed them by casting lots for them [Psalm 22:18]. (see Luke 23:34 AMP)

HOLY SPIRIT,

I am not a person, who judges those practicing such things, and does the same, because I will not escape the judgment of God. I do not despise the riches of the Father's goodness, forbearance, and longsuffering, knowing that the goodness of my Father leads me to repentance.
(see Romans 2:3-4 NKJV)

FATHER,

The Lord will go forth like a mighty man, You will rouse up Your zealous indignation and vengeance like a warrior; You will cry, yes, You will shout aloud, You will do mightily against my enemies.
(see Isaiah 42:13 AMP)

3

Your Relationship with Him
Prayers and Confessions

FATHER,
as my understanding of the realm of Your Kingdom increases so
will my participation in that realm. As I develop my faith, my area
of operation in the realm of God (the Kingdom) will expand and You
will entrust more to me.

LORD,
I want to know You better. As in any relationship, there must be a bond of
trust developed between two people. I sense that at times, You knew that
I was not ready for certain things that I thought should happen in my life.
I realize now that when I matured to a desired level, I could handle a lot
more than previously. You then revealed to me more of You and gave me the
desires of my heart. You have increased the bond
between us and my trust has grown.

HOLY SPIRIT,

three areas where honesty must be found are: in my heart, in my mind and in my relationships with the Trinity and others.

FATHER,

on the good ground are they, which in an *honest* and good heart, having heard the Word, keep It, and bring forth fruit with patience (Luke 8:15 KJV, emphasis added). I thank You that I am good ground and I yield to the Holy Spirit to water my Seed.

FATHER,

every believer is called to live the life described in Mark 11:23–26. More than I can even imagine is possible if I will only believe that the things I say will be done.

FATHER,

I speak out my faith! It is a part of my relationship with You. Jesus told me to speak to my mountains and I need to do it!

FATHER,

the key to my relationship with Jesus is to mature to the place of implementation into Your Kingdom activities. I became a co-laborer with Jesus in the Kingdom business. The Trinity has big plans for me!

FATHER,

I need to let the Spirit of Reality permeate me now as Your holy presence gives me revelation into the true meaning of my life. I confess my sins (shortcomings) and yield to what You have written about me in Heaven. I am transparent before You and allow You to lead and guide me. You love me so very much. Big things are in store for me because I trust in You.

FATHER,

I have been crucified with Christ; It is no longer I who live, but Christ lives in me; and the life which I now live in the flesh I live by faith in the Son of God, Who loved me and gave Himself for me (see Galatians 2:20).

JESUS,

I yield to Your Spirit, and I speak out and prophesy to my world. I bring correction to my circumstances as I yield and express the truth found in Your Word. I speak it out, and I see correction come. Everything in all of creation was made by Your words, is sustained by Your words, and responds to Your words (see Psalm 103:20).

JESUS,

You are asking me to accept Your forgiveness and allow You to cleanse me from a guilty conscience. If You say, "Your sins are forgiven," then they are! Getting this right is so important. You see my relationship with You as so important that You actually died for me. You love me! Let the healing flow now as I sense Your forgiveness take effect.

JESUS,

I am seed on good ground, which in an honest and good heart, having heard the word, keep it, and bring forth fruit with patience.
(see Luke 8:15 KJV)

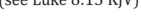

FATHER,

I avoid this, that no man should blame me in this abundance, which is administered by me: Providing for honest things, not only in the sight of the Lord, but also in the sight of men.
(see 2 Corinthians 8: 20–21 KJV)

HOLY SPIRIT,

I will dwell on whatsoever things are true, whatsoever things are honest, whatsoever things are just, whatsoever things are pure, whatsoever things are lovely, whatsoever things are of good report; if there be any virtue, and if there be any praise, think on these things.
(see Philippians 4:8 KJV)

JESUS,

You said a time will come, indeed it is already here, when the true (genuine) worshipers will worship the Father in spirit and in truth (reality); for the Father is seeking just such people as these as His worshipers. I am one of those worshippers and yield to the Holy Spirit continually.
(see John 4:23 NKJV)

JESUS,

You tell me to love You and keep Your commandments. Then, You will pray the Father, and He will give me another Helper, that He may abide with me forever—the Spirit of truth, Whom the world cannot receive, because it neither sees Him nor knows Him; but I know Him, for He dwells with me and will be in me. (see John 14:16-18 NKJV)

FATHER,

in front of Your throne there is also what looks like a transparent glassy sea, as if of crystal. And around the throne, in the center at each side of the throne, are four living creatures (beings) who are full of eyes in front and behind [with intelligence as to what is before and at the rear of them].
(see Revelation 4:6 NKJV)

FATHER,

Your wall is built of jasper, while the city [itself was of] pure gold, clear and transparent like glass. (see Revelation 21:18 NKJV)

HOLY SPIRIT,

You tell me to labour therefore to enter into that rest, lest any man fall after the same example of unbelief. For the Word of God is quick, and powerful, and sharper than any two-edged sword, piercing even to the dividing asunder of soul and spirit, and of the joints and marrow, and is a discerner of the thoughts and intents of the heart. Neither is there any creature that is not manifest in your sight: but all things are naked and opened unto your eyes with whom I have to do. Seeing then that I have a great high priest, which is passed into the Heavens, Jesus the Son of God, I hold fast my profession. For I have not a high priest which cannot be touched with the feeling of my infirmities; but was in all points tempted like as I am, yet without sin. I therefore come boldly unto the throne of grace that I may obtain mercy, and find grace to help in time of need.
(see Hebrews 4:11–16 KJV)

JESUS,

You said to me, "My grace is sufficient for you, for My strength is made perfect in [my] weakness." Therefore, most gladly I will rather boast in my infirmities, that the power of Christ may rest upon me.
(see 2 Corinthians 12:9 NKJV)

FATHER,

If I say that I have no sin, I deceive myself, and the truth is not in me. If I confess my sins, You are faithful and just to forgive me of my sins and to cleanse me from all unrighteousness. If I say that I have not sinned, I make You a liar, and Your Word is not in me.
(see 1 John 1:8-2:1 NKJV)

FATHER,
for though Jesus was crucified in weakness, yet He lives by the power of God. For I also am crucified in weakness with Jesus, but I shall also live with Jesus by the power of God.
(see 2 Corinthians 13:4 NKJV)

FATHER,
if then I was raised with Christ, seek those things that are above, where Christ is, sitting at the right hand of God. I set my mind on things above, not on things on the earth. For I died and my life is hidden with Christ in God.
(see Colossians 3:1–3 NKJV)

JESUS,
You said, "Whoever says to this mountain, 'Be removed and be cast into the sea,' and does not doubt in his heart, but believes that those things he says will be done, he will have whatever he says. Therefore I say to you, whatever things you ask when you pray, believe that you receive them, and you will have them. And whenever you stand praying, if you have anything against anyone, forgive him that your Father in Heaven may also forgive you your trespasses. But if you do not forgive, neither will your Father in Heaven forgive your trespasses."
(see Mark 11:23–26 NKJV)

FATHER,
Jesus said, "If you can believe, all things are possible to him who believes."
(see Mark 9:23 NKJV)

FATHER,
therefore if the Son makes you free, you shall be free indeed.
(see John 8:36 NKJV)

JESUS,

I repent of unbelief; for assuredly, You say to me, if you have faith as a mustard seed, you will say to this mountain, "Move from here to there," and it will move; and nothing will be impossible for you.
(see Matthew 17:20 NKJV)

FATHER,

You are the Lord, You do not change; that is why I am not consumed.
(see Malachi 3:6 AMP)

JESUS,

I shall receive power (ability, efficiency, and might) when the Holy Spirit has come upon me, and I shall be Your witness in Jerusalem and all Judea and Samaria and to the ends (the very bounds) of the earth.
(see Acts 1:8 AMP)

LORD,

I have been enlightened, I have consciously tasted the Heavenly gift and have become a sharer of the Holy Spirit, And have felt how good the Word of God is and the mighty powers of the age and world to come.
(see Hebrews 6:4-5 AMP)

JESUS,

"Blessed are those who are called to the marriage supper of the Lamb!'" And he said to me, "These are the true sayings of God." And I fell at his feet to worship him. But he said to me, "See that you do not do that! I am your fellow servant, and of your brethren who have the testimony of Jesus. Worship God! For the testimony of Jesus is the Spirit of Prophecy."
(see Revelation 19:9–10 NKJV)

4

When Heaven Arrives: Holy Spirit, Glory, and Angels Prayers and Confessions

Father,

I know that the Kingdom of God originated in Heaven. Heaven is a time-less realm that has always existed. It is not limited by distance, because it is in a different dimension than the earth. When this supernatural Kingdom comes in contact with the earth, anything not in line with the Kingdom will have to get out of the way or change. The Holy Spirit will convict the world of sin, righteousness, and judgment as part of this process. I fully yield to Your supernatural kingdom and choose to cooperate with it as an ambassador for You.

Lord,

When I yield to this Kingdom, the Holy Spirit will begin to reveal truth and conviction will come. Angel activity will increase as well because angels are the military branch of the Kingdom. God's glory will arrive where I am when there is submission and divine order in place.

Lord, You have appointed seasons for everything and we are entering into
the *Days of Heaven on Earth*!

JESUS,

You are the brightness of God's glory and the express image of His person,
and upholding all things by the word of His power, when You had by
Yourself purged our sins, sat down at the right hand of the
Majesty on high (see Hebrews 1:3).

FATHER,

it is not for me to become acquainted with and know what time brings [the
things and events of time and their definite periods] or fixed years and seasons (their critical niche in time), which You have appointed (fixed and
reserved) by Your own choice and authority and personal power. But I have
received power (ability, efficiency, and might) when the Holy Spirit came
upon me, and I shall be a witness in my town, state, and country;
to the ends (the very bounds) of the earth
(see Acts 1:7–8 AMP).

FATHER,

You have assigned the wonderful person called the Holy Spirit to teach me
how to walk successfully through this life and to tell me of things to come. I
will live the life for which I was designed. Because He is the Spirit of truth,
He will lead me along my true path. I make this promise from Jesus a reality.
Father, You sent the Helper, the Holy Spirit, in Jesus's name, He will teach
me all things, and bring to my remembrance all things that You said to me
(see John 14:26 NKJV).

FATHER,

as I begin to yield to the Holy Spirit and let go of my own ways, He will teach me to understand Your ways. He will make it possible for me to experience everything written about me in my Heavenly biography.

JESUS,

I make myself available for Your purposes and allow Heaven to be formed in me by praying in the Spirit.

JESUS,

You tell me the truth. It is to my advantage that You went away; for if You did not go away, the Helper would not have come to me; You said, "but if I depart, I will send Him to you. And when He has come, He will convict the world of sin, and of righteousness, and of judgment: of sin, because they do not believe in Me; of righteousness, because I go to My Father and you see Me no more; of judgment, because the ruler of this world is judged."
(see John 16:7–11 NKJV)

JESUS,

it is not for me to become acquainted with and know what time brings [the things and events of time and their definite periods] or fixed years and seasons (their critical niche in time), which the Father has appointed (fixed and reserved) by His own choice and authority and personal power. But I shall receive power (ability, efficiency, and might) when the Holy Spirit has come upon me, and I shall be Your witness in Jerusalem and all Judea and Samaria and to the ends (the very bounds) of the earth.
(see Acts 1:7–8 AMP)

JESUS,

You talked about the Comforter (Counselor, Helper, Intercessor, Advocate, Strengthener, Standby), the Holy Spirit, Whom the Father will send in

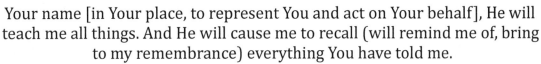

Your name [in Your place, to represent You and act on Your behalf], He will teach me all things. And He will cause me to recall (will remind me of, bring to my remembrance) everything You have told me.
(see John 14:26 AMP)

HOLY SPIRIT,

when You, the Spirit of Truth (the Truth-giving Spirit) comes, You will guide me into all the Truth (the whole, full Truth). For You will not speak Your own message [on Your own authority]; but You will tell whatever You hear [from the Father; You will give the message that has been given to You], and You will announce and declare to me the things that are to come [that will happen in the future].
(see John 16:13 AMP)

FATHER,

You instruct me about the spiritual gifts (the special endowments of supernatural energy). You do not want me to be misinformed. You said, "You know that when you were heathen, you were led off after idols that could not speak [habitually] as impulse directed and whenever the occasion might arise. Therefore I want you to understand that no one speaking under the power and influence of the [Holy] Spirit of God can [ever] say, Jesus be cursed! And no one can [really] say, Jesus is [my] Lord, except by and under the power and influence of the Holy Spirit. Now there are distinctive varieties and distributions of endowments (gifts, extraordinary powers distinguishing certain Christians, due to the power of divine grace operating in their souls by the Holy Spirit) and they vary, but the [Holy] Spirit remains the same. And there are distinctive varieties of service and ministration, but it is the same Lord [Who is served]. And there are distinctive varieties of operation [of working to accomplish things], but it is the same God Who inspires and energizes them all in all. But to each one is given the manifestation of the [Holy] Spirit [the evidence, the spiritual illumination of the Spirit] for good and profit. To one is given in and through the [Holy] Spirit [the power to speak] a message of wisdom, and to another [the power to express] a word of knowledge and understanding according to the same

[Holy] Spirit; To another [wonder-working] faith by the same [Holy] Spirit, to another the extraordinary powers of healing by the one Spirit; To another the working of miracles, to another prophetic insight (the gift of interpreting the divine will and purpose); to another the ability to discern and distinguish between [the utterances of true] spirits [and false ones], to another various kinds of [unknown] tongues, to another the ability to interpret [such] tongues. All these [gifts, achievements, abilities] are inspired and brought to pass by one and the same [Holy] Spirit, Who apportions to each person individually [exactly] as He chooses."
(see 1 Corinthians 12:1–11 AMP)

FATHER,

but the fruit of the [Holy] Spirit [the work which His presence within accomplishes] is love, joy (gladness), peace, patience (an even temper, forbearance), kindness, goodness (benevolence), faithfulness, Gentleness (meekness, humility), self-control (self-restraint, continence). Against such things there is no law [that can bring a charge]. And I who belong to Christ Jesus (the Messiah) have crucified the flesh (the godless human nature) with its passions and appetites and desires. If I live by the [Holy] Spirit, let me also walk by the Spirit. [If by the Holy Spirit I have my life in God, let me go forward walking in line, my conduct controlled by the Spirit.]
(see Galatians 5:22–25 AMP)

JESUS,

You are the one who gave these gifts to the Church: the apostles, the prophets, the evangelists, and the pastors and teachers. Their responsibility is to equip God's people to do Your work and build up the Church, the Body of Christ, until we come to such unity in our faith and knowledge of God's Son that we will be mature and full grown in the Lord, measuring up to the full stature of Christ.
(see Ephesians 4:11–13 NLT)

FATHER,

You said, "My Presence will go with you, and I will give you rest." Then he (Moses) said to You, "If Your Presence does not go with us, do not bring us up from here. For how then will it be known that Your people and I have found grace in Your sight, except You go with us? So we shall be separate, Your people and I, from all the people who are upon the face of the earth." So You said to Moses, "I will also do this thing that you have spoken; for you have found grace in My sight, and I know you by name." And Moses said, "Please, show me Your glory." Then You said, "I will make all My goodness pass before you, and I will proclaim the name of the LORD before you. I will be gracious to whom I will be gracious, and I will have compassion on whom I will have compassion." But You said, "You cannot see My face; for no man shall see Me, and live." And You said, "Here is a place by Me, and you shall stand on the rock. So it shall be, while My glory passes by, that I will put you in the cleft of the rock, and will cover you with My hand while I pass by. Then I will take away My hand, and you shall see My back; but My face shall not be seen."
(see Exodus 33:14–23 NKJV)

JESUS,

You are the brightness of His glory and the express image of His person, and upholding all things by the Word of His power, when You had by Yourself purged our sins, sat down at the right hand of the Majesty on high…
(see Hebrews 1:3 NKJV)

JESUS,

of the angels You say, "Who makes His angels spirits and His ministers a flame of fire." But to which of the angels have You ever said, "Sit at My right hand, till I make Your enemies Your footstool?" Are they not all ministering spirits sent forth to minister for those who will inherit salvation?
(see Hebrews 1:7, 13-14 NKJV)

5

PHASE ONE: REVELATION PRAYERS AND CONFESSIONS

———◦◆◦———

FATHER,

I always pray to You, the God of my Lord Jesus Christ, the Father of glory, that You may grant me a Spirit of wisdom and revelation [of insight into mysteries and secrets] in the [deep and intimate] knowledge of You, by having the eyes of my heart flooded with light, so that I can know and understand the hope to which You have called me, and how rich is Your glorious inheritance in the saints (Your set-apart ones), and [so that I can know and understand] what is the immeasurable and unlimited and surpassing greatness of Your power in and for me who believes, as demonstrated in the working of Your mighty strength, which You exerted in Jesus when You raised Him from the dead and seated Him at Your [own] right hand in the Heavenly [places], far above all rule and authority and power and dominion and every name that is named [above every title that can be conferred], not only in this age and in this world, but also in the age and the world which are to come. You have put all things under Your feet and have appointed Jesus the universal and supreme Head of the Church [a headship exercised throughout the Church] (Psalms 8:6), which is His Body, the fullness of Him Who fills all in all [for in that body lives the full measure of Jesus, Who makes everything complete, and Who fills everything everywhere with Himself]
(see Ephesians1: 17–23 AMP).

FATHER,

for this reason I bow my knees to You, the Father of our Lord Jesus Christ, from Whom the whole family in Heaven and earth is named, that You would grant me, according to the riches of Your glory, to be strengthened with might through Your Spirit in the inner man, that Jesus may dwell in my heart through faith; that I, being rooted and grounded in love, may be able to comprehend with all the saints what is the width and length and depth and height—to know the love of Jesus which passes knowledge; that I may be filled with all Your fullness. Now to You, Father, Who are able to do exceedingly abundantly above all that I ask or think, according to the power that works in me, to You be glory in the Church by Christ Jesus to all generations, forever and ever. Amen
(see Ephesians 3:14-21 NKJV).

HOLY SPIRIT,

I yield to the God of our Lord Jesus Christ, the Father of glory, that He may grant me a spirit of wisdom and revelation [of insight into mysteries and secrets] in the [deep and intimate] knowledge of Him, By having the eyes of my heart flooded with light, so that I can know and understand the hope to which He has called me, and how rich is His glorious inheritance in the saints (His set-apart ones), And [so that you can know and understand] what is the immeasurable and unlimited and surpassing greatness of His power in and for me who believe, as demonstrated in the working of His mighty strength, Which He exerted in Christ when He raised Him from the dead and seated Him at His [own] right hand in the Heavenly [places], Far above all rule and authority and power and dominion and every name that is named [above every title that can be conferred], not only in this age and in this world, but also in the age and the world which are to come. And He has put all things under His feet and has appointed Him the universal and supreme Head of the Church [a headship exercised throughout the Church], [Psalm 8:6.]Which is His body, the fullness of Him Who fills all in all [for in that body lives the full measure of Him Who makes everything complete, and Who fills everything everywhere with Himself].
(see Ephesians 1:17–23 AMP)

FATHER,

the earth was without form and an empty waste, and darkness was upon the face of the very great deep. The Spirit of God was moving (hovering, brooding) over the face of the waters. Now, you are moving on me (hovering, brooding) and have wonderful plans for my world.
(see Genesis 1:2 AMP)

FATHER,

You have unveiled and revealed the deep things by and through your Spirit, for the [Holy] Spirit searches diligently, exploring and examining everything, even sounding the profound and bottomless things of God [the divine counsels and things hidden and beyond man's scrutiny].
(see 1 Corinthians 2:10 AMP)

FATHER,

in many separate revelations [each of which set forth a portion of the Truth] and in different ways You spoke of old to [our] forefathers in and by the prophets, [But] in the last of these days You have spoken to us in [the person of a] Son, Whom You appointed Heir and lawful Owner of all things, also by and through Whom Jesus created the worlds and the reaches of space and the ages of time [He made, produced, built, operated, and arranged them in order]. Jesus is the sole expression of the glory of God [the Light-being, the out-raying or radiance of the divine], and Jesus is the perfect imprint and very image of [God's] nature, upholding and maintaining and guiding and propelling the universe by His mighty word of power. When Jesus had by offering Himself accomplished our cleansing of sins and riddance of guilt, He sat down at the right hand of the divine Majesty on high, [Taking a place and rank by which] Jesus Himself became as much superior to angels as the glorious Name (title) which He has inherited is different from and more excellent than theirs.
(see Hebrews 1:1–4 AMP)

FATHER,

Abraham waited patiently in faith and succeeded in seeing the promise fulfilled. It is very common for people to swear an oath by something greater than themselves, for the oath will confirm their statements and end all dispute. So in the same way, You wanted to end all doubt and confirm it even more forcefully to those who would inherit Your promises. Your purpose was unchangeable, so You added his vow to the promise. So it is impossible for You to lie for I know that Your promise and Your vow will never change! And now I have run into Your heart to hide myself in Your faithfulness. This is where I find Your strength and comfort, for You empower me to seize what has already been established ahead of time—an unshakeable hope! I have this certain hope like a strong, unbreakable anchor holding my soul to You. My anchor of hope is fastened to the mercy seat which sits in the Heavenly realm beyond the sacred threshold, and where Jesus, my Forerunner, has gone in before me. He is now and forever my Royal Priest like Melchizedek.
(see Hebrews 6:15-20 TPT)

FATHER,

if I was raised with Christ, I seek those things that are above, where Christ is, sitting at Your right hand. I set my mind on things above, not on things on the earth. For I died, and my life is hidden with Christ in You.
(see Colossians 3:1–3 NKJV)

6

Phase Two: Visitation Prayers and Confessions

Jesus,

visitation is when You come and manifest in a special way and spend time with me. As a friend Who visits, You share intimate information (revelation) but do not stay permanently for any extended period of time. Of course, I know You promise never to leave me or forsake me (Deuteronomy 31:6, John 14:18). The Holy Spirit is with me always. He may or may not manifest as strongly at times as in other special times. Thank You for not leaving me alone.

Holy Spirit,

I worship God; for the testimony of Jesus is the Spirit of Prophecy!
(see Revelation 19:10 NKJV)

Father,

visitation involves Jesus or the Holy Spirit coming and manifesting in a supernatural way. You are manifesting to the church and its individual members at various times.

42

HOLY SPIRIT,
You manifest with signs and wonders and miracles and gifts as You will.

JESUS,
You will come and be in our midst as we gather in Your name.

FATHER,
when I live my life within the shadow of the God Most High, my secret Hiding Place, I will always be shielded from harm! How then could evil prevail against me, or disease infect me? You send angels with special orders to protect me wherever I go, defending me from all harm. If I walk into a trap, they'll be there for me and keep me from stumbling! I'll even walk unharmed among the fiercest powers of darkness, trampling every one of them beneath my feet! For here is what the Lord has spoken to me, "Because you have delighted in Me as My great lover, I will greatly protect you. I will set you in a high place, safe and secure before My face. I will answer your cry for help every time you pray, and you will find and feel My presence even in your time of pressure and trouble. I will be your glorious Hero and give you a feast! You will be satisfied with a full life and with all that I do for you. For you will enjoy the fullness of my salvation"
(see Psalm 91:9-16 TPT, emphasis added).

FATHER,
You require something of me, and so the visitation phase is where You are going to start to show me parts of You that You have not shown to me previously. It's going to change me, and it's also going to affect my relationships with others, because they may not be comfortable,
but they will be influenced for change.

Jesus, with visitation, I will have to change, because whatever You give to me, You require something back. You are revealing Yourself to me and want to spend more time with me. My face is changing with each visitation.

HOLY SPIRIT,
Thou hast granted me life and favour, and thy visitation
hath preserved my spirit
(see Job 10:12 KJV).

HOLY SPIRIT,
I hear you tell me to be strong and of good courage, do not fear nor be afraid of them; for the LORD your God, He is the One who goes with you. He will not leave you nor forsake you.
(see Deuteronomy 31:5 NKJV)

JESUS,
You said, "I will not leave you orphans; I will come to you."
(see John 14:18 NKJV)

FATHER,
You honored Joseph and remembered to visit his relatives. He said to his brethren, "I am going to die. But God will surely visit you and bring you out of this land to the land He swore to Abraham, to Isaac, and to Jacob [to give you]." (see Genesis 50:24 AMP)

FATHER,
You said, "Shall I hide from Abraham [My friend and servant] what I am going to do?" (see Galatians 3:8) ... And the You said, "Because the shriek [of the sins] of Sodom and Gomorrah is great and their sin is exceedingly grievous, I will go down now and see whether they have done altogether

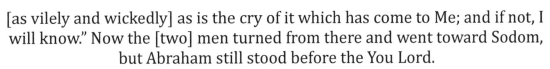

[as vilely and wickedly] as is the cry of it which has come to Me; and if not, I will know." Now the [two] men turned from there and went toward Sodom, but Abraham still stood before the You Lord.
(see Genesis 18:17, 20–22 AMP)

JESUS,

You said, "Again I say to you that if two of you agree on earth concerning anything that they ask, it will be done for them by My Father in heaven. For where two or three are gathered together in My name, I am there in the midst of them." (see Matthew 18:19–20 NKJV)

HOLY SPIRIT,

they were all filled with You and began to speak with other tongues, as the You gave them utterance. (see Acts 2:4 NKJV)

FATHER,

when I live my life within the shadow of You, the God Most High, my secret Hiding Place, I will always be shielded from harm! How then could evil prevail against me, or disease infect me? You send angels with special orders to protect me wherever I go, defending me from all harm. If I walk into a trap, they'll be there for me and keep me from stumbling! I'll even walk unharmed among the fiercest powers of darkness, trampling every one of them beneath my feet! For here is what You have spoken to me, "Because you have delighted in me as my great lover, I will greatly protect you. I will set you in a high place, safe and secure before my face. I will answer your cry for help every time you pray, and you will find and feel my presence even in your time of pressure and trouble. I will be your glorious Hero and give you a feast! You will be satisfied with a full life and with all that I do for you. For you will enjoy the fullness of my salvation!"
(see Psalm 91:9-16 TPT)

FATHER,

Thou hast granted me life and favour, and Thy visitation hath preserved my spirit. (see Job 10:12 KJV)

7

Phase Three: Habitation Prayers and Confessions

Father,

there is a place where the Spirit of the Lord can take me to where my whole spiritual house has been framed by revelation from God, and then it has been ornamented with visitation and now I am being occupied with habitation. And it's permanent.

Holy Spirit,

habitation is a place where the Father has won me over and my face is glowing and it doesn't bother me. Jesus has taken me to a place where I have so much in common with Him. I have become like Him. My face is glowing.

Father,

1 Corinthians 14:14-16 explains, "For if I pray in a tongue, my spirit prays, but my understanding is unfruitful. What is the conclusion then? I will pray with the spirit, and I will also pray with the understanding." Therefore, I

pray and sing in the Spirit and with my understanding. I will sing with the spirit, and I will also sing with the understanding.

FATHER,

it's time to fall in love. When I grow intimate with You, my desires become Your desires. If I do not desire the things You want, it's time for a healthy dose of "Heavenly Reality" from the Spirit of Truth.

FATHER,

I make the decision to love You with all my heart and obey all that You command, You are able to move in with me. Obviously the criterion has been met through the precious Blood of Jesus that was shed. It's just a matter of time now, so I might as well give up on resisting any longer. You are much too strong for me and You know I want to be caught by You. Up until this point, I have been pursuing You by asking for Revelation. You accommodate me through the Holy Spirit and answer my prayers based on the Apostle Paul's prayers in the letters to the Ephesians, and Colossians (see Ephesians 1:17–23; Colossians 1:9-23). You begin to frame me as a house would be framed using beautiful beams of Revelation, revealing Yourself through Your Word to me. Next, You begin to come to me through Visitation. As I enter this phase, I desire to know You even more. The more You visit the more I desire for You to visit. It gets to where I want You to stay! I pursue You until Habitation comes.

FATHER,

You turn around in the middle of me pursuing You and You let me catch You. Then, You begin to pursue me and I can't escape You. You see, Jesus You are irresistible to me, but what I did not know was that I became irresistible to You and now You pursue me! I am in Habitation!

FATHER,

Therefore, I am in Christ, I am a new creation; old things have passed away; behold, all things have become new. Now all things are of You, who has reconciled me to Yourself through Jesus Christ, and has given me the ministry of reconciliation, that is, that You, in Christ, are reconciling the world to Yourself, not imputing their trespasses to them, and has committed to me the word of reconciliation. Now then, am an ambassador for Christ, as though You were pleading through me: I implore you on Christ's behalf, be reconciled to God. For You made Jesus who knew no sin to be sin for me, that I might become the righteousness of God in You.
(see 2 Corinthians 5:17-21 NKJV)

FATHER,

whenever Moses went out to the Tent of Meeting, all the people would get up and stand in their tent entrances. They would all watch Moses until he disappeared inside. As he went into the tent, the pillar of cloud would come down and hover at the entrance while You spoke with Moses. Then all the people would stand and bow low at their tent entrances. Inside the Tent of Meeting, You would speak to Moses face to face, as a man speaks to his friend. Afterward Moses would return to the camp, but the young man who assisted him, Joshua son of Nun, stayed behind in the Tent of Meeting.
(see Exodus 33:8-11 NLT)

FATHER,

when Moses came down the mountain carrying the stone tablets inscribed with the terms of the covenant, he wasn't aware that his face glowed because he had spoken to the You face to face. And when Aaron and the people of Israel saw the radiance of Moses' face,
they were afraid to come near him.
(see Exodus 34:29-30 NLT)

FATHER,

that old system of law etched in stone led to death, yet it began with such glory that the people of Israel could not bear to look at Moses' face. For his face shone with the glory of God, even though the brightness was already fading away. Shouldn't I expect far greater glory when the Holy Spirit is giving life? If the old covenant, which brings condemnation, was glorious, how much more glorious is the new covenant, which makes me right with God! In fact, that first glory was not glorious at all compared with the over-whelming glory of the new covenant. So if the old covenant, which has been set aside, was full of glory, then the new covenant,
which remains forever, has far greater glory.
(see 2 Corinthians 3:7-11 NLT)

HOLY SPIRIT,

all things are legitimate [permissible—and I am free to do anything I please], but not all things are helpful (expedient, profitable, and whole-some). All things are legitimate, but not all things are constructive [to character] and edifying [to spiritual life].
(see I Corinthians 10:23 AMP)

JESUS,

You say, "Come to Me, all you who labor and are heavy laden, and I will give you rest. Take My yoke upon you and learn from Me, for I am gentle and lowly in heart, and you will find rest for your soul. For My yoke is easy and My burden is light."
(see Matthew 11:28-30 NKJV)

FATHER,

for as the heavens are higher than the earth, So are Your ways higher than my ways, And Your thoughts than my thoughts.
(see Isaiah 55:9 NKJV)

JESUS,

for if I pray in a tongue, my spirit prays, but my understanding is unfruitful. What is the conclusion then? I will pray with the spirit, and I will also pray with the understanding. I will sing with the spirit, and I will also sing with the understanding.
(see 1 Corinthians 14:14-16 NKJV)

JESUS,

I, who once was alienated and enemies in my mind by wicked works, yet now you have reconciled in the body of Your flesh through death, to present me holy, and blameless, and above reproach in His sight—if indeed I continue in the faith, grounded and steadfast, and are not moved away from the hope of the gospel which I heard, which was preached to every creature under heaven, of which I, became a minister.
(see Colossians 1:19-23 NKJV)

HOLY SPIRIT,

now therefore I am no more strangers and foreigners, but fellow citizens with the saints, and of the household of God; And am built upon the foundation of the apostles and prophets, Jesus Christ himself being the chief corner stone; In whom all the building fitly framed together groweth unto an holy temple in the Lord: In whom I also am built together for an habitation of God through the Spirit.
(see Ephesians 2:19-22 KJV)

FATHER,

now I saw heaven opened, and behold, a white horse. And He who sat on him was called Faithful and True, and in righteousness He judges and makes war. His eyes were like a flame of fire, and on His head were many crowns. He had a name written that no one knew except Himself.
(see Revelation 19:11-13 NKJV)

8

ENOCH, THE BRIDE, AND THE CHURCH AGE PRAYERS AND CONFESSIONS

JESUS,
the powers of the coming age are mentioned in the book of Hebrews.
Thank You that I have been enlightened, have tasted the Heavenly gift, have
become a partaker of the Holy Spirit, and have tasted the good Word of God
and the powers of the age to come. I will not fall away from You, the Son of
God, and put You to an open shame
(see Hebrews 6:4-6 NKJV).

HOLY SPIRIT,
I worship God; for the testimony of Jesus is the Spirit of Prophecy
(see Revelation 19:10 NKJV)!

FATHER,
I realize that the resurrection power dwelling in me wants to raise people
from the dead. I can spiritually raise people from the dead just by testifying

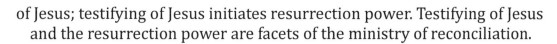

of Jesus; testifying of Jesus initiates resurrection power. Testifying of Jesus and the resurrection power are facets of the ministry of reconciliation.

FATHER,

I am an ambassador for Christ, as though God were pleading through me: I implore people on Christ's behalf, *"Be reconciled to God."* I do this because "God made Jesus, Who knew no sin to be sin for me, that I might become the righteousness of God in Him" (see 2 Corinthians 5:21).

FATHER,

I get the extra oil in my lamp now. I recognize the extra oil is for tomorrow when I awaken. I'll be a thousand years ahead in my supply. I know Holy Spirit that You are giving me the abundant supply of oil I need to burn and be a light. I receive more than enough and burn brightly in and for You. Oil is being delivered by the Holy Spirit daily to my doorstep from Heaven.

FATHER,

it is impossible for those who were once enlightened, and have tasted the Heavenly gift, and have become partakers of the Holy Spirit, and have tasted the good Word of God and the powers of the age to come, if they fall away, to renew them again to repentance, since they crucify again for them-selves the Son of God, and put Him to an open shame.
(see Hebrews 6:4-6 NKJV)

FATHER,

John fell at his feet to worship him. But the angel said to him, "See that you do not do that! I am your fellow servant, and of your brethren who have the testimony of Jesus. Worship God! For the testimony of Jesus is the Spirit of Prophecy."
(see Revelation 19:10 NKJV)

HOLY SPIRIT,

for the love of Christ compels me, because I judge thus: that if One died for all, then all died; and He died for all, that those who live should live no longer for themselves, but for Him who died for me and rose again. Therefore, from now on, I regard no one according to the flesh. Even though I have known Christ according to the flesh, yet now I know Him thus no longer. Therefore, if i am in Christ, I am a new creation; old things have passed away; behold, all things have become new. Now all things are of You, who has reconciled me to Himself through Jesus Christ, and has given me the ministry of reconciliation, that is, that You were in Christ reconciling the world to Yourself, not imputing my trespasses to me, and has committed to me the word of reconciliation. Now then, I am an ambassador for Christ, as though God were pleading through me: I implore you on Christ's behalf, be reconciled to God. For You made Jesus who knew no sin to be sin for me, that I might become the righteousness of God in Jesus. (see 2 Corinthians 5:14-21 NKJV)

FATHER,

as were the days of Noah, so will be the coming of the Son of Man.
(see Matthew 24:37 AMP)

FATHER,

but of that day and hour no one knows, not even the angels in Heaven, nor the Son, but only You. (see Mark 13:32 NKJV)

HOLY SPIRIT,

as the Scripture says, eye has not seen and ear has not heard and has not entered into my heart, [all that] You have prepared (made and keeps ready) for me who love you [who hold You in affectionate reverence, promptly obeying You and gratefully recognizing the benefits You has bestowed].
[Isaiah 64:4; 65:17.] (see 1 Corinthians 2:9 AMP)

CONCLUSION

Jesus, You can take me to a place where I'm way beyond my years. I'm way beyond what people have planned for me. I'm way beyond what I have planned for you. I way beyond any and all of what can be imagined by the carnal mind. I have the capacity to do the impossible, and the only reason why is because I have allowed Jesus to talk to me and influence me as a person. I let the next step be the one that places me in your Days of Heaven on Earth!

CPSIA information can be obtained
at www.ICGtesting.com
Printed in the USA
LVHW100739070620
657581LV00009B/540

9 781498 469685